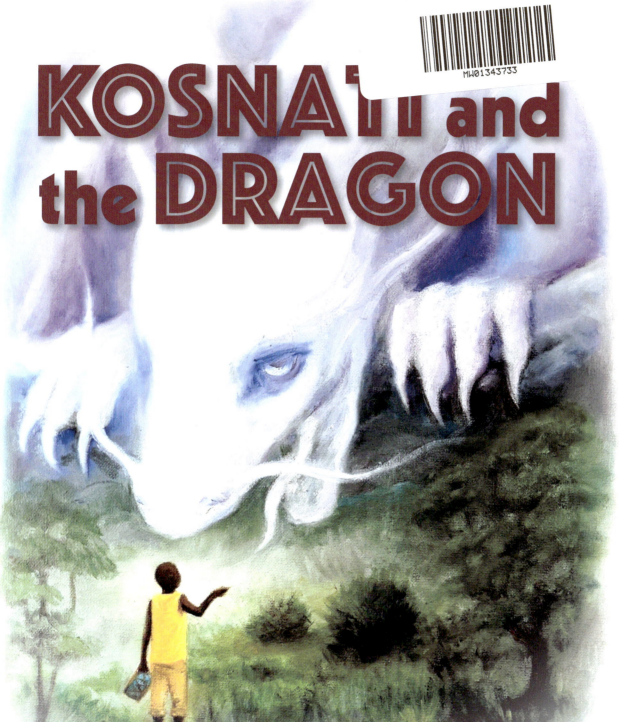

KOSNA'II and the DRAGON

retold by **Leni Smith Covington**

illustrated by **Tessa Guze**

KENYON AVENUE PRESS
Durham, North Carolina

Kosnati and the Dragon
ISBN: 978-1-7366593-4-2 softcover
ISBN: 978-1-7366593-5-9 ebook
Library of Congress Control Number: 2022900868

Copyright ©2022 by Leni Smith Covington
All Rights Reserved.

No part of this book may be reproduced in any written, electronic, recording, or photocopy form without the prior written permission of the publisher, except for the inclusion of brief quotations in a review.

Publisher's Cataloging-in-Publication data
Names: Covington, Leni Smith, author. | Guze, Tessa, illustrator.
Title: Kosnati and the Dragon / retold by Leni Smith Covington; illustrated by Tessa Guze.
Description: Durham, NC: Kenyon Avenue Press, 2022. | Summary: A dragon regularly visits Kosnati's village and causes great damage from lashes of wind and rain. Kosnati challenges the dragon with creative problem solving.
Identifiers: LCCN: 2022900868 | ISBN: 978-1-7366593-4-2 (paperback) | 978-1-7366593-5-9 (epub)
Subjects: LCSH Dragons--Juvenile fiction. | Tales--South Africa. | South Africa--Juvenile fiction. | Folklore--South Africa. | BISAC JUVENILE FICTION / Fairy Tales & Folklore / Country & Ethnic
Classification: LCC PZ7.1.C686 Ko 2022 | DDC 398.2--dc23

Illustrations by Tessa Guze
Copyedited by Lucy Long Ivey
Book Design by Bob Schram, Bookends Design

Printed in the United States of America

Published by
KENYON AVENUE PRESS
Durham, NC
kenyonavenuepress.com • info@kenyonavenuepress.com

Dedicated to

Leni's family:

My Three African-American Nephews
Matt Adkins, Eric James McDew, and Anthony Martin McDew

Their Wives
Anne Marie Adkins, Liz Vail, and Amanda McDew

Their Children
Cameron Adkins and Kaylen Adkins
Ashley McDew, Rosemary McDew, and Eric Devray McDew
Tyler McDew and Braxton McDew

And their Mother
Rosemary Elizabeth Smith McDew

Tessa's family:

My daughters,
Claire and Elleke,
who always help me scare my dragons away.

Once upon a time there was a little boy called Kosnati. He lived with his mother in a small village under the Drakensberg Mountains in KwaZulu-Natal. He helped his mother by fetching water from the river and by looking after the goats during the day.

Sometimes Kosnati's friends would go with him down to the river. They would find clay on the riverbank. Then they would sit together and model birds out of the clay.

In those days, the people of the village grew afraid when they saw the sky darken with heavy gray clouds in early autumn. They would hear the roar of the dragon behind those clouds. They would see flashes of fire from the dragon's nostrils coming down from those clouds! If the dragon was very angry, he would come right over the mountains, bringing great lashings of wind and rain with him. The wind and rain would blow over the villagers' huts and flood their land.

Often they would lose some of their animals in the floods. Sometimes a child or elderly person would be trapped in the floods. Sometimes one of them would get struck by the dragon's flashing fire.

And so it happened that one autumn morning, Kosnati and his friends went with the goats down to the river. They were sitting on the riverbank, making little clay birds. Suddenly, many swallows flew low over their heads.

Kosnati was so excited about the swallows' first flight! He went running along the riverbank, jumping up and flapping his hands as if he would fly. "How I would love to fly like a bird!" he exclaimed to his friends. Then he sat down to make a swallow out of clay.

The swallows were also trying to tell the children that a storm was coming. It was not just any storm, but a storm brought by the dragon! The sun began to darken, and the children all looked up. They saw the approaching blue-black clouds over the mountains.

"I had better get home and fetch my mother's calabash to get water before the storm comes!" Kosnati shouted to his friends above the distant roar of the dragon. "You take the goats and the clay birds into the rocky cave!" He rushed back to tell his mother about the storm. He wanted to let her know that he was going to fetch some water.

"Oh, Kosnati, look how dark it is!" cried Umama. "It is too late, my boy. It is safer to stay home."

"Umama, I must go. You know that sometimes it can storm for many days. We will be in trouble without water to wash and cook. I must go!" said Kosnati.

Umama called to her mother, Kosnati's Ugogo, to try to persuade Kosnati to stay. Kosnati would not listen, even to Ugogo. Umama then went to the villagers to ask them to help her. Some were too busy, some were too sick, and some just didn't care.

"If Kosnati wants to be stubborn, he will just have to learn a lesson, won't he?" they said.

And so Kosnati prepared to return to the river. He knew that he might have to face the dragon. He made a plan about what to take with him: He strapped his drum across his shoulder, he tucked Umama's calabash under his arm, and he picked up a big stone along the way.

In his absence, Kosnati's friends had become frightened because it had grown much darker very quickly. They hurriedly gathered up the clay birds and herded the goats inside the cave. They were hiding there when at last they saw Kosnati come down to the river with his drum, his mother's calabash, and the big stone.

Then, suddenly, the fierce dragon came over the mountain. His nostrils were shooting flames, and he made loud, thundering growls. The children were so scared, they couldn't look. They lowered their heads and continued to work on their clay birds, praying and hoping all the while that Kosnati would be saved.

Kosnati saw the dragon coming over the mountain with his loud roaring. Kosnati put up his little hand and shouted, "STOP!" The dragon was so surprised, he stopped in his tracks. He became quiet and waited to see what this brave little boy wanted.

"Before you eat me," Kosnati bargained, "I have a big chunk of cheese for you. Here! Open your jaws, and I will throw it in!"

The dragon did as he was told. Kosnati threw the big stone into the dragon's jaws. The dragon brought his teeth together sharply. When he bit into the stone, quite a few teeth broke. The dragon grew very angry as he spit the teeth onto the ground.

"Wait!" exclaimed Kosnati. "Before you eat me, just promise that you will eat me only once!"

"Ha, ha," laughed the dragon. "What a silly boy! I only NEED to eat you once." He opened his jaws, and Kosnati jumped inside with his drum. The dragon swallowed Kosnati whole, very satisfied with himself.

But then something very strange began to happen. The dragon's stomach began to ache, and he felt very queasy. You see, Kosnati had taken his drum with him and had begun to play his drum and dance!

Boom, boom, dubi, dubi, boom.
Boom, boom, dubi, dubi, boom!

"Oh," moaned the dragon. "What is happening to me? Maybe this meal of the little boy does not agree with me!"

And so he opened his great jaws, and Kosnati jumped out. The dragon was so amazed at the little boy's bravery that tears came to his eyes and began to fall in great splashes on the ground.

As the tears fell, a beautiful green light grew around the form of the dragon. His scales began to fall off, and the misty form of a young woman emerged.

The young woman shimmered with light and beauty. "You have released me from my bondage, and now I can show my true form. And so that you and the others may always be reminded of your bravery, take what used to be my teeth, and plant them in the ground. When there is no rain, remember to water them. And you will see a wonder." In a fine mist she spread her veils over the valley and gently brought rain to the valley.

Kosnati's friends had watched in amazement as their dear friend emerged from the dragon's jaws. They saw how the dragon changed its form. Just then, the birds they had made out of clay flew out of the cave into the soft, misty rain. The birds circled the mysterious shimmering young woman as she floated across the valley.

The boys ran out to Kosnati, and together they herded the goats back to the village. Kosnati's mother rejoiced when she saw him. She was afraid that she had lost her son forever!

Even the villagers who had not cared what would happen to Kosnati became curious when they saw him return. They watched as Kosnati began to dig the soil. They watched him plant the dragon's teeth. They watched as, at first, little green shoots appeared.

They watched the stems sprout leaves. They watched the stems grow taller and taller until, at last, they were taller than Kosnati and his friends.

To this day, the people of that village continue to hand the story of Kosnati down to their children and grandchildren. Each year, when they see the sunflowers blooming in the autumn, they are reminded of the young boy's bravery, courage, and love for his family and village.

About the Author

LENI SMITH COVINGTON has been both a Waldorf school teacher and a public school teacher for 30-plus years. She has taught classes in infant, toddler, and parent education, and has been a classroom teacher in Nursery through Grade 5, both in-class and homebound. She has further taught students as a reading specialist, and as a special education and an ELL teacher. Ms. Covington founded two private Waldorf preschools and has mentored Waldorf teachers in Xian, China, and Raleigh, North Carolina. She has two sons, and five grandchildren whom she loves reading aloud to.

Ms. Covington's first book, a retelling of *The Shoemaker and the Elves* (2021), won the second-place 2021 CIPA (Colorado Independent Publishers Association) EVVY award for children's books for ages 5 to 9.

About the Illustrator

TESSA GUZE studied visual art at Durham School of the Arts and then at Moore College of Art and Design, where she focused on children's book illustrations and discovered oil painting, her preferred medium. She taught art and English in India and then in South Korea for several years and now teaches at a Waldorf preschool in the mornings. She works on portrait commissions in the evenings. She is mother to two little girls who both adore picture books, reading, and making lots of art.

Advance Praise for Kosnati and the Dragon

With more than 30 years as an educator, I can say that Kosnati's story is one that will appeal to children of all ages. The detailed and explicit language helps to paint a picture in the reader's mind that is enhanced by the beautiful illustrations. This story is a perfect complement to texts utilized in elementary and middle school classrooms that acknowledge and study diverse cultures. It is also an entertaining read-aloud that will enhance vocabulary building for students, especially English language learners of all ages.

–ANNE MARIE ADKINS, MA, Principal
Herbert Akins Middle School, Fuquay-Varina, NC

We enjoyed reading this book with our four-year-old son. It had great lessons of love and bravery in it, and the story was easy to follow. We like books that help our son to develop character traits like compassion and strength to overcome adversities. A nice addition to our children's book collection!

–AMANDA MCDEW, MSW, Proud Parent of Braxton, Salt Lake City, UT

In this retelling of the indigenous fairy tale Kosnati and the Dragon, the protagonist, Kosnati, a Black South African of Zulu ethnicity, shows the reader tenets of courage, fortitude, and creativity. The wonderfully crafted text allows the powerful unfolding of imagination in children. I recommend this retelling of Kosnati and the Dragon as an important addition to the inclusive library since it embraces the intersections of race, ethnicity, and universal attributes.

–MONIQUE F. BRINSON, MS, Founding Head of School Center of Gravity Academy
Pre-K through 8, Pleasant Hill, CA

Student of Yang's Martial Arts Association (YMAA, Boston, MA, USA),
trained in Drakensberg, South Africa (the cradle of civilization)

Presenter at Waldorf 100 Festival, Berlin, Germany, in honor of the Centennial Anniversary of Waldorf Education, Stuttgart, Germany (the birthplace of Waldorf education)